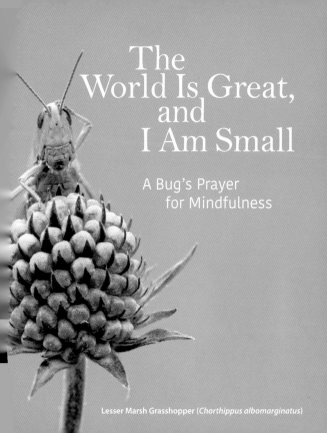

The World Is Great, and I Am Small

A Bug's Prayer for Mindfulness

Lesser Marsh Grasshopper (*Chorthippus albomarginatus*)

Cairns Birdwing Butterfly (*Ornithoptera eu*

The World Is Great, and I Am Small

A Bug's Prayer for Mindfulness

BRADLEY TREVOR GREIVE

New York Times Bestselling Author of *The Blue Day Book*

Andrews McMeel Publishing®

a division of Andrews McMeel Universal

Other Books by Bradley Trevor Greive

Juvenile Broad-Winged Bush Katydid (*Scudderia pistillata*)

Schoenherr's Blue Weevil (*Eupholus schoenherri*)

Dedicated to the memory of
Dr. Douglas Frew Waterhouse
(1916–2000)

A man so beloved and admired that he very
nearly made entomology sexy.

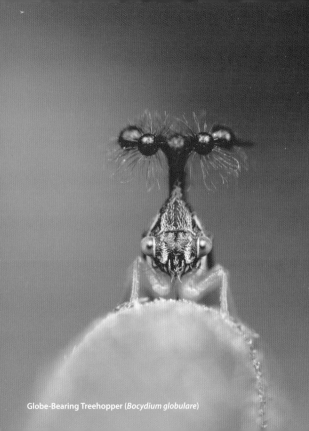

Globe-Bearing Treehopper (*Bocydium globulare*)

*"If one truly loves nature
one finds beauty everywhere."*

—Vincent van Gogh

Lychee Shield Bug (*Chrysocoris stolli*)

Let me start by confessing that I'm probably not the most religious person you're ever likely to meet. When I was a little boy, I dreaded going to church. As soon as my tiny buttocks made contact with the unforgiving hardwood pew, my parents would initiate extreme containment measures. My father would sit on the aisle to block my escape route while my mother would hand me pencil and paper, and with a loving/ pleading/warning gaze she would ask me to draw an animal species starting with the letter A and continue the exercise for each letter of the alphabet. I took this zoological art task seriously and it usually kept me quiet and still throughout the preacher's seemingly interminable sermon. But when it didn't, I would be

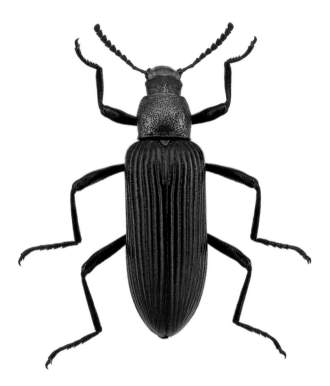

Darkling Beetle (*Strongylium cupripenne*)

sent outside to explore the churchyard hedges where I would gleefully stuff cicadas, snails, and lizards into the pockets of my best clothes. I knew I'd be in serious trouble when the church service was over, but it was almost always worth it. To this day, whether I'm tracking brown bears or searching for unusual beetles, I'm always happiest when I'm immersed in nature. It's little wonder that when deep spiritual matters occupy my thoughts, I have always felt more comfortable in a forest than in a cathedral.

In my mind, God is Nature. If you wish to be humbled and inspired, regardless of your religious beliefs or lack thereof, simply stand before a mountain range, a thundering waterfall, or a towering redwood . . . or just turn over a small rock and see what you find underneath. I guarantee you a joyous revelation . . . unless you find a venomous snake, in which case I promise mixed feelings.

I honestly wasn't the worst student in my religious studies classes; however, I generally suffered through unimaginative scripture lessons until the day I suddenly sat up with such radiant attentiveness that my drowsy teacher stumbled back in alarm. We were discussing the book of Exodus, specifically the ten plagues sent by God to compel Pharaoh to free the Israelites. I wanted to know why God chose to send not one but three plagues of insects, namely lice, flies, and locusts. Sure, in hindsight each species proved an excellent, plague-worthy choice, but keep in mind God could have theoretically sent a million tigers, elephants, polar bears, or bag-pipers to give the recalcitrant Pharaoh (and self-proclaimed god-king) a deafening wake-up call. But instead God humbled the most powerful nation on Earth with teeny-tiny, harmless insects just to show what he is capable of . . . kind of like a heavyweight boxing champ knocking

Passionvine Hopper Nymph (*Scolypopa australis*)

Common Cockchafer Beetle a.k.a. Doodlebug
(*Melolontha melolontha*)

out his cocky challenger with bad breath (probably not the best metaphor). Perhaps God also wanted to teach us all a lesson in humility by demonstrating that the least of us, and indeed the most often overlooked, are every bit as consequential as the greatest of our number, if not more so.

I love insects, especially beetles. In much the same way that a small yet perfect diamond is far more valuable than a truckload of coal, insects are so dense with life and dazzling purpose that they often make far more celebrated wildlife species seem rather dull by comparison. To watch a spider spin a web, a bee give precise navigation coordinates by dancing, a Hercules Beetle carry one thousand times its own weight, or a Spittlebug Nymph knit a suit of armor out of bubbles is to witness the divine beauty of an impossible, effortless thing. Having said that, I must make it clear that spiders are not actually insects (like scorpions, they are arachnids, and are as distinct from butterflies as badgers are from canaries), but I hope you get my point. The unfathomable complexity and superpower abilities that are unique to these tiny living gems are beyond remarkable.

Today we know of one million different insect species and, based on annual rates of discovery, have good reason to believe there could be more than thirty million species yet to be found. Insects currently make up 80 percent of all animal species and account for 20 percent of the earth's terrestrial animal biomass: a staggering one-fifth of the mass of all living creatures that walk, crawl, skip, or fly (including bison, hippos, hummingbirds, dingoes, ferrets, lemurs, fainting goats, and thoughtless vulgarians who block your view at the theatre by wearing hats indoors).

Earth is, by definition, an insect realm. Numbering 7.5 billion, our own species is one of the most successful to draw breath; however, insects outnumber us by at least two hundred million to one. In case that doesn't impress you, consider this: for every single human being there are twenty-one tons of insects. This is why grandiose insect clergy have every right to assume that God made this planet especially for *their* kind and granted *them* dominion over everything. To put it another way, aliens traveling to Earth for an intergalactic diplomatic mission would not make their way to the White House in Washington, D.C., or to Zhongnanhai in Beijing, but instead would touch down in Amazonia and respectfully ask to speak with His Excellency, the Chief Beetle, or Her Royal Majesty, the Queen Ant.

But it is not just the number and variety of insects that shivers and delights our oversized primate brains—it's how essential insects are for our species to survive. It was reported that when the celebrated

British scientist J. B. S. Haldane was asked by a theologian what he had deduced about God from his lifelong study of natural history, Haldane replied as follows: "If one could conclude as to the nature of the Creator from a study of creation, it would appear that God has an inordinate fondness for stars and beetles." I can think of no better pairing.

Stars are the great celestial engines that manufacture the fundamental elements from which the Earth and its inhabitants are composed. And by consuming and transforming organic waste into vital nutrients, insects create the conditions in which life on Earth can be sustained. One could therefore argue that starlight and beetle poop (known as frass) are the Lord's secret ingredients.

As the famed American biologist E. O. Wilson once said, "If we were to wipe out insects alone on this planet, the rest of life and humanity with it

Golden Scarab Beetle (*Plusiotis resplendens*)

would mostly disappear from the land. Within a few months." Of course, E. O. Wilson may be guilty of exaggerating just a little in order to make us all feel better—many scientists believe it would take far less than a few months for human life to come to a pungent, shuddering halt if insects ceased to exist, perhaps just a week or three (roughly the same amount of time as if the Sun were suddenly turned off). More than three-quarters of all flowering plants, which include our largest food crops and also the grasses and forage plants that our livestock eat, require pollination by insects, so therefore most of us would starve to death and the rest would soon fall prey to swarm-clouds of bacteria or drown in heaped mounds of our own fetid waste. Such a cheery thought, I know. Conversely, if all humanity were wiped out, insects almost certainly wouldn't notice . . . except perhaps for Dust Mites and Bedbugs that feast on flakes of our dead skin and suck our blood while we sleep, and frankly no one would miss them either.

I appear to have taken this preface to a rather dark place, so please allow to me lighten the mood as we move toward the conclusion. Insects are truly fascinating and beautiful, and one way or another each and every species contributes to our happiness and survival. With a few notable exceptions, most insects live for less than a year—some only a few months or a few weeks, and in the case of adult Mayflies, less than twenty-four hours. Despite such a short lifespan, insects do more to sustain all life on Earth than you or I ever will. Each time you see an insect it should serve to remind you that every second counts.

With so much to do and so little time in which to do it, not to mention all manner of giant creatures paying them no consideration other than when trying to kill and eat them, I can well imagine an insect feeling

Lappet Moth (*Trabala pallida*)

exhausted and defeated and perhaps suffering from acute stress disorder. Which is why I find it inspiring that busy little bugs rally to their duty every day and night, regardless of how badly the odds are stacked against them. You may scoff at this. In the past it was thought that insects had no brains, no memories, no capacity to learn, no ability to make tools, and no feelings of pain or pleasure. But more recent studies prove that such sweeping statements serve only to discredit human intelligence, for we were utterly wrong about everything. Honeybees and Cockroaches may have only one million neurons in their respective brains, as opposed to our eighty billion, but they are intelligent, sentient creatures nonetheless.

Being small and delicate doesn't make you stupid or weak, or mean that your cherished plans and best labors don't matter. Which is just as well for us because in the context of our planet, our solar system, and our universe, we are far tinier and far more fragile than the smallest Aphid Nymph.

In the prayer for mindfulness that follows, a selection of remarkable insects stand in for each of us when we are feeling overwhelmed, helpless, inconsequential, and invisible. The bug's earnest prayer reminds us we are never truly alone and that help is always at hand. And just as every tiny insect has hidden capabilities that will amaze even the most cynical observer, so too each of us can draw upon our faith, our knowledge, and our self-belief to tap into strengths we never knew we had in order to overcome that which might otherwise seem impossible.

I truly believe that each and every one of us has a purpose we are uniquely capable of achieving. We may be small, but we are an important part of something monumental, and what we do, say, think, and feel has the power to change the world. So whether you inhale air through your nose and mouth, or through tiny spiracles along your armored abdomen, I encourage you to exalt in every single breath—because life truly is an incredible gift, and your life matters to all of us.

Hummingbird Hawk-Moth (*Macroglossum stellatarum*)

The World Is Great, and I Am Small

A Bug's Prayer for Mindfulness

Oh, many-legged Lord,

The world is great and I am small.

Amid a billion trillion insects living on this planet,

I sometimes feel like I am utterly alone.

Without Your loving guidance, I would be completely lost and afraid.

And, frankly, when facing this kind of existential crisis, I generally look a little goofy.

Lanternfly (*Pyrops candelaria*)

The fact is, on my own,

I'm not nearly as intimidating as the world
around me.

I need You by my side to make it through today.

And so I ask that You raise up my voice like a
Green Grocer Cicada,[1]

That my prayer might reach unto the heavens.

Amidst the chaos and confusion of the twenty-first century,

Please help me be as still as a Stick Insect.[2]

Giant Malaysian Leaf Insect (*Phyllium giganteum*)

For only then can I appreciate the incredible beauty and wonder that surrounds me.

Like a Dung Beetle,[3] may I gaze upon all the crap life has strewn in my path

And see it for the incredible opportunity that it is.

Scarab Beetle (*Scarabaeus sacer*)

When beset by daily perils,

I ask that you turn your benevolent antennae and compound eyes toward me

To calm my heart and fortify my resolve,

Praying Mantis (*Mantis religiosa*)

So that I may be as fearless as an Antlion[4]

And as tough as an Ironclad Beetle.[5]

Grant me the strength of a Leafcutter Ant[6]

Leafcutter Ant (*Atta cephalotes*)

So I might happily bear any burden.

I am aware that we live in uncertain times,

But please don't let my fear of the unknown make me someone who always expects the worst.

I ask, instead, that You let Your light shine through me, like a Tortoiseshell Beetle,[7]

So that everything I do and say brightens the faces of those around me.

Let me be a window to a better world.

Tortoiseshell Beetle (*Aspidimorpha miliaris*)

Help me to heed the Sugarbag Bee's[8] example,

That creativity, kindness, and generosity are the most powerful weapons of all.

And to appreciate that, like a Common Rose
Butterfly,[9]

All that seems magnificent once began as an
unremarkable and fragile thing

And was made stronger and more beautiful by
countless acts of love and courage.

Peanut-Head Bug (*Fulgora laternaria*)

Grant me the quiet dignity of the
Peanut-Head Bug.[10]

Make me immune to what unkind people say
about me behind my back.

Don't let me be impressed or cowed by the
superficial or be inclined to pursue popularity
for its own sake.

Encourage me to search for meaning and
substance, and to undertake noble endeavors
that are not motivated by the approval of others.

Ultimately it is not how the world sees me but
how You see me that truly matters.

Please bestow upon me the well-deserved self-confidence of a Bombardier Beetle[11] and help me unleash the greatness within.

Through You, all things are possible, so I never wish to underestimate just how freaking awesome I can be.

Bombardier Beetle (*Brachinus alternans*)

But Lord, however good I feel about who I am and what I stand for,

Please prevent me from turning up my nose at anyone,

Never let me be a snob or a bigot of any kind.

However pitifully small I may be, I always wish to be bigger than that.

Help me to embrace the dazzling breadth of our planet's biodiversity

And welcome those whose appearances and habits are different from my own,

For we are all connected.

From the Goliath Beetle[12] to the Fairyfly,[13]

Each of the many millions of insect species on this earth are Your creation

And, as such, are forever worthy of celebration.

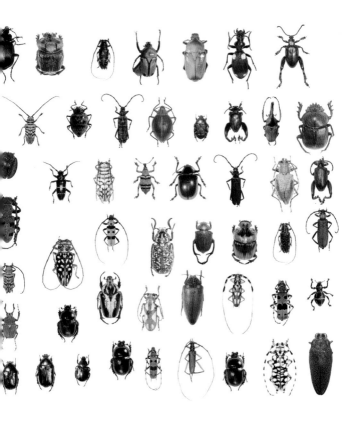

Make me mindful of the fact that,

While not everyone has my best interests at heart,

I have no real enemies other than those I make
for myself.

Like the Large Blue Butterfly[14] and the Red Ant,

My future depends on the kindness of strangers.

Oh Sublime Arthropod, I know my time on earth is painfully brief.

Please make me as swift as a Tiger Beetle[15]

So that I do not waste a single picosecond.

When I take up the work for which I was chosen,

May I be as intelligent as the brainiest Termite[16]

And as industrious as the busiest Honeybee.[17]

Violet Carpenter Bee (*Xylocopa violacea*)

Make me as selfless and heroic as the
Paper Wasp,[18]

For like them I am here to serve others—

The health and well-being of my family and
friends

Is more important than my own.

German Wasp (*Vespula germanica*)

Please bless my ears with the hearing of a Greater Wax Moth,[19]

That I might be attentive to your guidance

And listen carefully to the hopes and dreams of those around me.

Gypsy Moth (*Lymantria dispar dispar*)

I ask for the foresight of the Morpho Butterfly's[20] ultraviolet receptors,

So that I may prepare for difficult days to come

And save my loved ones from the firestorm of strife and torment.

Please reforge my spirit to resemble a
Charcoal Beetle[21]

So that I might help bring forth new life and
new happiness

From the ashes of tragedy and misfortune.

No matter what challenges lie ahead,

However long the day and dark the night,

Let my heart be as light as a Pygmy Moth.[22]

Your world is rich in abundance and I need so little to be truly happy.

Please make me content with what I have

And help me share your blessings with those less fortunate than myself.

Brown Rhinoceros Beetle (*Xylotrupes gideon*)

Everyone I will ever meet hungers for love and acceptance

And thirsts for greater knowledge and understanding.

Help me guide them to Your living Word.

European Red Wood Ant (*Formica polyctena*)

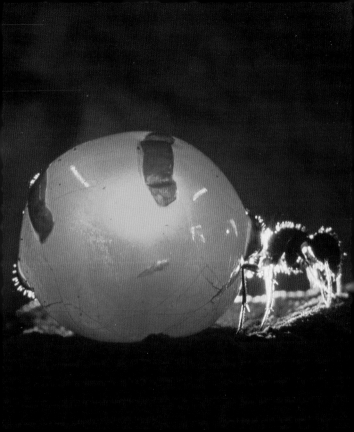

Please make me as generous as a Honeypot Ant.[23]

Let me be a source of joy for others.

Let my faith sustain them, just as Your love sustains me.

But please, oh Great Insect Lord, if you should grant me any of these gifts,

Help me to remain humble.

We both know that walking on water doesn't make me special.

Don't let me ever forget how small I am

Or that I am part of something wonderful

That is so much bigger than myself.

Help me embody the undying gratitude of an ordinary Fly,[24]

So that I fully appreciate that there is nothing ordinary about being alive:

That every atom of my being is marvelous and sacred,

That freedom of mind and body should never be taken for granted,

Black-Headed Cardinal Beetle (*Pyrochroa coccinea*)

That Your way is perfect, even if this world is not,

That every dawn contains a promise of new
happiness and greater purpose

And therefore my every conscious moment is a
blessing.

Southeastern Lubber Grasshopper (*Romalea microptera*)

Above all, Omnipotent Invertebrate,
I pray you grant me the vision of a Dragonfly,[25]

That I might see my place in the universe for
what it truly is:

A tiny but precious miracle.

I humbly ask these things in the name of the Head,

And of the Thorax,

Japanese Jewel Beetle (*Chrysochroa fulgidissima*)

And of the Abdomen.

Amen.

European Rhinoceros Beetle (*Oryctes nasicornis*)

Notes

1   The Green Grocer Cicada (*Cyclochila australasiae*), from southeastern Australia, is one of the world's loudest insects and in fact one of the loudest living creatures, period. During the summer mating season, the male's high-pitched drumming call often exceeds 120 decibels, which is roughly the same volume as Luciano Pavarotti singing "Nessun Dorma" while wielding a chainsaw.

2   Stick Insects and Leaf Insects, also known as Phasmids, come in countless shapes and sizes, and can be found on every continent except Antarctica. Some species are very petite, such as the Timema Walking Stick (*Timema californica*), which is barely half an inch long. However the biggest species, a giant stick insect found in southern China (*Phryganistria chinensis Zhao*),

Azure Damselfly (*Coenagrion puella*)

Giraffe Weevil (*Trachelophorus giraffa*)

is over two feet in length, making it the longest insect on the planet. The one thing every Stick Insect has in common is the ability to mimic their surroundings with extraordinary accuracy, which makes them almost invisible to predators. If you want me to go into full Earth Mother Wisdom Mode, then I would say that in order to enjoy a peaceful existence they have become one with their environment.

3   The most famous Dung Beetle (*Scarabaeus sacer*) is a Scarab Beetle from northern Africa and southern Europe. As its name suggests, the Dung Beetle's life revolves around poop. Not just any poop, mind you. Dung Beetles have special poop-sensing antennae and choose their poop as carefully as a brie-fondling cheese snob at Zabar's; they are poop connoisseurs, if you will. Male and female Dung Beetles usually fall in love when they bump into each other while flying

to the very same pile of fresh poop, and there and then they decide to have an impromptu dinner date. First they work together to shape the poop into a ball that is many times their bodyweight (one species of Dung Beetle has been measured pulling well over one thousand times its mass, which is like an average human being picking up two battle tanks). Using their specially adapted back legs, the Dung Beetles roll their massive poop-sphere to a romantic location where it is buried safely underground and then eaten at a leisurely pace. When the female Dung Beetle is ready to breed, she chooses especially fine and moist herbivore poop to create a large hollow ball. After laying a single egg inside, she seals up the opening with poop, a dash of saliva, and plenty of love (I'm guessing), and waits. The adorable Dung Beetle larva hatches two days later and feeds on the nutritious poop walls of their nursery before entering the pupa phase. A month or two later, a fully formed Dung Beetle emerges from the ball and digs its way to the surface, ready to devour all the crap the world can throw at it. Observing the emergence of baby Dung Beetles, ancient Egyptians considered them to be magical creatures that epitomized Creation itself. Likewise, the way Dung Beetles pushed balls of dung across the ground was used as a way to describe how Khepri, a subordinate deity to Ra (the mighty Egyptian Sun God), moved the morning sun up into the heavens, bringing light, warmth, and life itself into the world each day.

[4]   Antlions (*Distoleon tetragrammicus*) are actually Lacewing larvae—but while they grow up to be slender, delicate flying insects as adults (bloodthirsty ballerinas, if you will), as juveniles they are brutal ambush predators. The Antlion hunting technique is quite extraordinary. They lie in wait, completely

concealed, at the base of an almost perfectly conical pit-trap crafted in fine sand. As insects walk around the edge, they slip down the slope of the pit, and the Antlion, alerted to their presence by the tumbling grains of sand, lunges up from the bottom to seize them in its mighty jaws, not unlike a great white shark surging from the depths. Though George Lucas has never said as much, every entomologist alive today assumes the creator of *Star Wars* was directly inspired by Antlions to create the dreaded Sarlacc in *Return of the Jedi*. While we are speculating, I have often thought that one of the key reasons that Antlions are so ferociously brave is that they do not have an anus and do not poop, and therefore they can never soil their underpants in the heat of battle.

5   The Ironclad Beetle (*Zopherus nodulosus haldemani*) is incredibly tough and almost impossible

Predaceous Diving Beetle (*Cybister fimbriolatus*)

Atlas Moth Caterpillar (*Attacus atlas*)

to kill, thanks to its extra thick and superhard exoskeleton. Ironclad Beetles cannot fly, as their outer wing coverings (called elytra) are fused together like plates of armor. These wood-boring armored cars are so tough that the entomologists who study them cannot push a pin through a dead specimen to attach it to a display mount for preservation and must instead use an electric drill.

6   The Leafcutter Ant (*Atta cephalotes*) is a highly organized species of ant found living in tropical America from Bolivia to Mexico. Long lines of these ants are easily spotted in the rainforest as each member carries freshly cut sections of leaves back to their nest, which can be twenty feet wide and twenty feet deep and contain a population far greater than Chicago. You might assume that the ants eat these leaves, but this is not the case at all. Leafcutter Ants are fungus eaters

Puss Moth Caterpillar (*Cerura vinula*)

and, more importantly, fungus farmers. They take the fresh leaves and use them to feed their underground fungus gardens to ensure a healthy crop, much in the same way a human farmer cultivates a field.

[7] The Tortoiseshell Beetle (*Aspidimorpha miliaris*) is a small, flattish leaf-eating beetle that, when viewed from above, is almost circular in appearance because its exoskeleton on the abdomen and thorax extends out beyond the body and head proper, creating a transparent shield. When threatened, the Tortoiseshell Beetle clamps down on a leaf surface, somewhat like a barnacle, with its head and legs fully covered by the hard halo of additional chitin, making it far more difficult for predators to dislodge and eat it. Apart from being very beautiful, the Tortoise Beetle family, found in Africa and southeast Asia, is an especially interesting one because some members can change

color beneath their transparent outer covering and also because their larvae are covered in dangerous-looking spikes and thus look and behave very differently to their parents—think Charlie Sheen and Martin Sheen.

8   The Sugarbag Bee (*Tetragonula carbonaria*) is an Australian native bee species, not too much larger than a housefly. They produce delicious honey, but unlike regular Honeybees, they do not sting. They are not aggressive by nature, and when hostile intruders attack their spiral-shaped nests, they deter them by swarming as one to form a dynamic, defensive cloud— similar to a flash mob, or the dance-fighting scenes in *West Side Story*. If push comes to shove, Sugarbag Bees settle their differences by wrestling.

9   There is nothing "common" about the Common Rose Butterfly (*Pachliopta aristolochiae*), an exquisite

black, white, and crimson Swallowtail Butterfly found throughout much of Asia and Australasia. This gorgeous creature was first described by the legendary Danish entomologist Johan Christian Fabricius in 1775, the same year in which the brilliant and beloved English novelist Jane Austen was born.

[10] The Peanut-Head Bug or Alligator Bug (*Fulgora laternaria*) is nothing like what it appears to be. Viewed from above, its huge head resembles that of a snake or lizard, and in conjunction with its startling wing spots, its intimidating appearance generally dissuades most would-be predators. However, the Peanut-Head Bug's jaws are not powerful. In fact, it can't bite at all because its mouth is actually a small tube designed specifically to consume plant sap. Nevertheless, according to Colombian folklore, if you are bitten by a Peanut-Head Bug, you will certainly die unless you have sex within

Peacock Katydid (*Pterochroza ocellata*)

twelve hours. This is obviously and hilariously false, but before you pick up a Peanut-Head Bug in order accelerate your carnal urges, be aware that, like a skunk, it can spray a terrible smelling substance that will put off even the most passionate lover for a lot longer than twelve hours.

11   In terms of raw firepower, no other insect comes close to the five-hundred-member Bombardier Beetle family. Like the Peanut-Head Bug, Bombardier Beetles also have a horrible-smelling spray in their defensive arsenal, but their version has a *lot* of extra kick. Equipped with special internal tanks that store volatile liquid chemical fuel, these small ground beetles can instantly initiate a powerful and extremely caustic exothermic chemical reaction that reaches 212°F and blasts out streams of blistering liquid and vapor at 735 lethal pulses per second. The tip of the beetle's

abdomen—their butt-mounted liquid flamethrower/ Gatling gun, if you will—can swivel 270 degrees to dish out a devastating thermal smackdown in almost any direction. Bottom line: do not sneak up behind a Bombardier Beetle as a joke, don't let them borrow your favorite jeans, and don't sit anywhere near them at the movies if they are watching *The Fly*.

12   The Goliath Beetle (*Goliathus goliatus*), a Scarab Beetle species from equatorial Africa, is the world's biggest and heaviest beetle. In its larval form, weighing in at well over 4 ounces (roughly twice the weight of a Blue Jay), the Goliath Beetle is also the world's heaviest insect. But curiously, just like the Bald Eagle, it actually loses weight as it matures and therefore ultimately yields the insect heavyweight title to the Giant Weta of New Zealand, which tops the record scales at just over 2.5 ounces.

True Bug (*Pephricus paradoxus*)

13   Fairyflies are the smallest members of the wasp family and also the world's smallest known insects, period. The *Dicopomorpha echmepterygis* species from Costa Rica is the smallest of them all; the blind male of this species measures considerably less than one one-thousandth of an inch, which is roughly the same size of a paramecium and half the size of an amoeba. Put another way, you could fit fifteen Fairyflies on the head of a pin, which is to say these little guys are so small that we humans never notice them. Fairyflies specialize in eating the eggs of other insects, and as a result they have been successfully used to reduce the numbers of rampant agricultural pests in the United States, French Polynesia, and South Africa, proving once again that you don't have to be big to be a big deal.

14   Sadly, the Large Blue Butterfly (*Phengaris arion*) went extinct in the United Kingdom in 1979, but now

this iconic species is back thanks to an excruciatingly difficult and rather brilliant reintroduction program led by David Simcox and Jeremy Thomas. The key to their plan was recognizing the extraordinary relationship that exists between the Large Blue Butterfly and an especially generous species of Red Ant called *Myrmica sabuleti*. Ants and butterflies normally don't get along very well, in large part because ants like to eat butterflies as well as the eggs and caterpillars that would have become butterflies. But in this case, it's all rather wonderfully back to front. Three weeks after the butterfly larvae hatch, they deliberately tumble off their flower petal crib and fall onto the ground, where they are picked up by foraging parties of Red Ants. The ants carry the babies home to an underground nursery, deep inside their nest, where they raise the butterfly grubs as their own. In truth, the baby butterflies take advantage of their hosts, eating far more than their share (and often eating the ant larvae in the nursery as well). The pampered caterpillars spend nine months underground before pupating and finally leaving their ant hosts to emerge into the glorious sunshine as Large Blue Butterflies. In summary, if there were no Red Ants, there would be no Large Blue Butterflies.

[15]   Tiger Beetles are not just one of the world's fastest insects, they are one of the fastest animals on Earth relative to their size. One flightless species of Australian Tiger Beetle (*Cicindela eburneola*) can run at speeds of almost 4.5 miles per hour, which doesn't sound that impressive until you realize this equates to an astonishing 171 body-lengths per second. To put this pocket-predator's athletic performance in context, the world's fastest mammal, the cheetah, can hit a top speed in excess of sixty miles per hour. However this only equates to sixteen body-lengths per second. And

Leaf Beetle (*Trichochrysea hirta*)

the world's fastest human can't even reach a top speed of twenty-eight miles per hour, which works out to be a rather pitiful nine body-lengths per second. Doing the math, this means that the Australian Tiger Beetle has a relative top speed of over 650 miles per hour! This result means that the Tiger Beetle would have held the (relative) world land speed record until 1983, when the Scottish pilot and entrepreneur Richard Noble drove his turbojet engine-powered car, Thrust 2, to 714 miles per hour on the Black Rock Desert in Nevada. By the way, the current world land speed record, set by British fighter pilot Andy Green in 1997, is 763 miles per hour . . . which is incredible and yet not out of reach for an especially dedicated Tiger Beetle who's fond of squats and crunches and lives to race.

16   Pest control companies like to paint Termites as literal home-wreckers in order to peddle their

toxic chemicals. However, the greater truth is that Termites are gifted architects and master builders. Numerous Termite species from northern Australia and southern Africa (including *Macrotermes bellicosus*) erect towering high-rise structures measuring as much as thirty feet tall and forty feet wide. These buildings are not just monumental in scale, they are also carefully and specifically designed to address the challenges of an extremely harsh environment: scorching droughts, high winds, and raging floodwaters. It may surprise you to learn that termite mounds are not primarily accommodation blocks but instead feature complex ventilation and air conditioning systems to ensure the comfort and health of the millions of residents living below ground level. In effect, these spectacular structures, which can be composed of several tons of earth, are huge artificial lungs. And keep in mind that these extraordinary respirating spires were designed and built by tiny bugs using only their saliva and grains of dirt, one mouthful at a time.

¹⁷ The heroic efforts made by Honeybees (*Apis mellifera*) to put food on our plates cannot be overstated. Just about every major crop you can think of relies on Honeybee pollinators in order to flourish. Worker bees labor from sunup to sundown, with the veteran forager team pushing themselves harder and harder to keep the hive supplied with nectar, pollen (a.k.a. "bee bread"), plant resin (for repairs), and water. Forager bees will sometimes shutdown from exhaustion midflight and fall asleep on a flower before rallying and continuing on for the sake of their hive family. In at least one recorded case, Honeybees have flown nectar-gathering missions of fourteen miles on their tiny glass-paper wings, collectively scouring an area

of over 250,000 acres. For an average human being to match this feat, relative to body mass, he or she would have to make eighteen return trips to the Moon in one day. If that isn't humbling, then I don't know what is.

[18]   Paper Wasp species, such as the Golden Paper Wasp (*Polistes fuscatus*) found throughout Central America and North America, are highly social insects that display many similar behaviors to bees, such as sending out foraging teams to gather food and building materials to support the nest. One key behavior is completely reversed, however. Junior Paper Wasps do all the foraging while the older, stronger wasps stay back to defend the nest. Paper Wasps are famous for the courage and ferocity they display when their nests are attacked by predators or rivals. Vespid counterattacks are especially savage if the nest contains eggs or juveniles. Unlike other eusocial insects (such

as bees, ants, and termites), the Paper Wasp queen is not a pampered and bloated egg-laying machine, but a resolute and fearless leader. The Paper Wasp queen is actually the most active and dangerous nest defender when duty calls; she will drive her venomous stinger into any foe and will lay down her life to protect her offspring if needed. In many ways, she is akin to the much-feared Briton warrior queen Boudicca, who led her Iceni tribe to a series of bloody victories against the Roman invaders, before finally being defeated in the Battle of Watling Street in 61 CE.

[19]   In 2013, scientists at the University of Strathclyde in Scotland proved the Greater Wax Moth (*Galleria mellonella*) was capable of hearing ultrasonic frequencies of up to three hundred kilohertz, a feat that, quite frankly, was previously thought impossible. This level of aural sensitivity places Greater Wax Moths in a

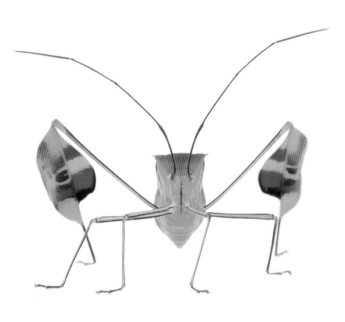

Flag-footed Bug (*Anisocelis flavolineata*)

league of their own; their hearing range is one hundred and fifty times better than humans, six times better than dogs, and twice as good as dolphins and the next most gifted moth, the Gypsy Moth (*Lymantria dispar*). In other words, the Greater Wax Moth's hearing is far better than any recorded living creature. And this is just as well, because the silver medal for the world's best listener goes to insectivorous bats that use echolocation to catch and eat moths. Bats can hear just over two hundred kilohertz in order to lock onto their flying prey in the pitch-black void of night. In this instance, however, the Greater Wax Moth can hear the bat coming before the bat even knows the moth is there, allowing the bat's would-be dinner the chance to escape the far larger, faster, and stronger predator.

[20]   The most famous Blue Morpho Butterfly species, the Menelaus Blue Morpho (*Morpho menelaus*), was

named in 1758 by Swedish zoologist Carl Linnaeus, who is considered the father of modern taxonomy. Linnaeus chose this name in homage to Menelaus, the belligerent king of ancient Sparta and the disgraced husband of legendary beauty Helen of Troy. Why? We can't be sure. However, Linnaeus had a wicked sense of humor, so perhaps in this case he wanted the male to be the ravishingly beautiful one in the relationship. From a practical point of view, Linnaeus classified more than thirteen thousand plant and animal species in his lifetime and he needed to get new names from somewhere, so why not mine the Greek classics he loved so dearly? Nomenclaturist trivia aside, there are many interesting things about the Morpho Butterfly that are worthy of mention. For example, this stunning blue butterfly is not really blue—its famous iridescent blue color is not the result of actual blue pigmentation, but merely an amazing light effect produced by

Panda Ant (*Euspinolia militaris*)

reflective nanostructures in each of the countless microscopic scales on its wings. Put simply, these tiny scales are to butterflies what feathers are to birds, and even though these scales might appear to be specks of fine dust if you rubbed any off on your fingers, when viewed under a microscope you would see they are almost perfect rounded rectangles, all arrayed in neat rows like tiles on a roof. In the Morpho Butterfly's case, each individual scale is essentially colorless. However, an electron microscope reveals a series of precise angular mirrors in several layers that work together to cancel out light with long wavelengths (yellows, oranges, and reds) and to reflect and amplify the very short wavelengths that encompass the blue and blue-green colors as well as ultraviolet (which we can't see, but the Morpho can). Dominant male Morpho Butterflies can be very territorial and will harass and chase off other males, but thanks to their remarkable ultraviolet reflecting wings and ultraviolet sensitive eyes, the butterflies can see each other a long way away and sense trouble coming, even deep within the dense and dimly lit rainforest, thus avoiding an unpleasant and potentially injurious encounter. One final thing that may surprise you about the elegant Morpho is that they don't consume nectar like most butterflies, but instead prefer to drink the dank liquid inside rotten fruit, which in many cases has fermented thanks to the tropical heat, thereby converting the fructose into ethanol (alcohol). Even though the butterflies can get a buzz from sipping their jungle cocktails, their characteristically jerky and unpredictable flying motion is not the result of the aviator being drunk, but because their wings are disproportionately large compared to their tiny bodies.

Leaf-footed Bug (*Sundarus tropicalis*)

[21]   You really wouldn't know it by looking at it, but the rather drab Charcoal Beetle (*Melanophila consputa*) is actually a member of the glittering jewel beetle family (Buprestidae). But whatever they lack in looks, Charcoal Beetles more than make up for with smarts. Insects have been around for some four hundred million years, and throughout that time they have been in an intimate relationship with trees—cohabitating, fighting, nurturing each other, consuming each other . . . it's complicated. During their larval stage, Charcoal Beetles, like most jewel beetles, are wood-boring insects. However, tree bark contains tough defenses to prevent newly hatched grubs from munching their way inside, which is why Charcoal Beetles only lay their eggs on trees that have just been in a fire, or in most cases, are still burning. Rushing to a forest fire to lay your eggs on defenseless trees when all other insects are flying away is both a cunning and very

brave way to beat your competition (assuming you don't get killed), but that isn't the most amazing thing about Charcoal Beetles. In order to identify potential breeding sites as soon as possible, Charcoal Beetles have special infrared detectors mounted behind their second set of legs (or in their second set of armpits, depending on how you view beetle anatomy) that can sense fires from eighty miles away or farther. This ability is so remarkable that scientists are trying to replicate this little beetle's biological fire detector to create thermal sensors that would provide early warning and increased safety for humans in countless domestic and industrial situations.

22   Pygmy Moths (a.k.a. Midget Moths) from the Nepticulidae family are the smallest moths in the world, with wingspans ranging from half an inch to less than one tenth of an inch. One nepticulid species

from the Democratic Republic of the Congo, first identified and collected by Dr. Steve Heydon from the University of California, Davis, measures only three one-hundredths of an inch, which is the size of the period at the end of this sentence.

23   The Australian Honeypot Ant (*Camponotus inflatus*) is the best friend you could ever have if you were trying to survive in the harsh Australian Outback. These unusual ants are a little like bees in that they store water and nectar away for future use. But instead of keeping their vital supplies in their nest, specific members (called plerergates or repletes) store these precious liquids inside their own bodies; gorging themselves until their abdomens swell up like transparent glass marbles or tiny golden Christmas decorations. Eventually the repletes get so huge they can't move and simply hang from the ceiling of the

Jewel Wasp (*Hedychrum niemelai*)

nest until another ant is hungry. Then the hungry ant strokes the replete's antennae to let them know they want to eat, and the replete vomits up the stored nectar into the hungry ant's mouth. It may not sound like the most appealing drive-through dining experience, but in fact Honeypot Ants are sweet and delicious and are considered a delicacy by many Australian Aboriginals from the Western Desert. Having eaten Green-Tailed Weaver Ants myself, which I found tangy and refreshing, I'd love to try some Honeypot Ants for dessert.

[24]   There are approximately one million species of true flies (from the order Diptera) and none of them ever feel ordinary. And why should they? According to entomologists at North Carolina State University, flies may have the greatest economic impact of any insect species, for better or for worse. Yes, they destroy some plants and spread over one hundred different

diseases to humans and livestock, but they also pollinate flowering plants, consume waste, and control other nasty pests. Plus, they can fly upside down, which is super cool. Finally, here's some interesting trivia for you: Mosquitoes, Gnats, and Midges are all true flies, but Dragonflies, Damselflies, and Mayflies are not.

25   Humans with perfect vision see images as combinations of three different primary colors: red, green, and blue. As described by Catherine Brahic in *New Scientist*, "This is thanks to three different types of light-sensitive proteins in our [retinas], called opsins." Dragonflies, however, have as many as thirty opsins and can therefore see ten times as many different colors. Plus, the Dragonfly, which specializes in daytime flight, can also see ultraviolet light and doesn't need to wear Ray-Ban Aviators to handle polarized light bouncing off of reflective surfaces such as glass, water, and bald heads.

Just as impressive, the Dragonfly's huge compound eyes each have some thirty thousand photoreceptor facets, thus delivering thirty thousand pictures for a truly comprehensive view of, well, almost everything. Put this all together and you have extremely precise vision that makes your high-definition television look like a drawing made with gray crayons. It is this spectacular visual acuity, along with the Dragonfly's powerful wings, that enables it to be the most gifted pilot on Earth. Forget what you saw in *Top Gun*; the Dragonfly can reach speeds of over thirty-five miles per hour, which in relative mass terms is over one hundred thousand times faster than a fighter jet. Dragonflies are also able to stop, execute 9G turns, or change course into any of six directions almost instantaneously in order to take down a tasty mosquito. Hunting Dragonflies are successful in 95 percent of their attacks, making them the undisputed ace of aces and the most effective predator on Earth.

True Weevil a.k.a Snout Beetle (*Cholus cinctus*)

Green Sweat Bee (*Agapostemon texanus*)

Acknowledgments

It's not every day that I call my publisher to propose a book that is inspired, in part, by Edward Gorey, John Donne, and Monty Python, but that was certainly the case with this particular volume. Suffice it to say I offer my heartfelt thanks to Patty Rice, my editor at Andrews McMeel Publishing, for taking me seriously and for not hanging up the phone. I also wish to express my gratitude and admiration for her talented team in Kansas City who have realized my curious vision so beautifully.

Sincere thanks are also due to the gifted photographers who have contributed stunning images to this project—I'd like to make special mention of David Chambon, in France, for answering my e-mails in the middle of the night; Bill Morgenstern, who delivered images while roaming between Texas and Canada; renowned Carcinologist (and my favorite atheist), Chris Lukhaup, in Germany, who gifted me my Moby Dick in the form of the elusive Panda Ant; and my dear friend, BBQ demigod and fellow armadillo-wrangler Jay Smith, in southeast Georgia.

As is my custom, I wish to acknowledge my benevolent literary agent and publishing god Sir Albert Zuckerman, who has tolerated my obsession with wildlife and wild places for a very long time. When I told Al I wanted to write a prayer of invocation from a beetle's point of view, it seemed entirely reasonable to him. Just as when my wife and I asked him to be the first Jew to be ordained as a nondenominational Christian minster so he could officiate our wedding. Al is as comfortable with his faith as he is making peerless predinner cocktails. It's an essential part of who he is, and on a daily basis, usually around 7:00 p.m., he uses the wisdom God has given him to make the world a far happier place.

For my own part, I have every reason to remain humble. In over forty years of searching, I have not discovered a single new species of insect, despite this feat being achieved by others roughly ten thousand times a year, every year. Nevertheless I feel blessed to fail at this particular life goal if pursuing it means I get to spend more time in the great outdoors in a state of euphoric wonderment.

Above all, I am grateful for the love and support of my extraordinary wife, Amy—a woman so remarkable that our first kiss made me believe in God again.

B.T.G.

About the Author

Bradley Trevor Greive AM, was born in Tasmania, though he lived abroad with his family for most of his childhood in Scotland, Wales, England, Hong Kong, and Singapore. After graduating from the Royal Military College, BTG served as a paratrooper platoon commander in the Australian Army. Upon leaving the military, he began a career in publishing as a cartoonist and has since gone on to become one of the world's most successful humor authors, with global sales now in excess of 30,000,000 copies across 115 countries. A semi-indestructible adventure sportsman, certified cosmonaut, and a Polynesian rock-lifting champion, BTG is also a wildlife expert and television personality. In the course of his many travels, he has been attacked by woolly monkeys, fruit bats, porcupines, reindeer, and fairy penguins, and has so far endured seventeen surgeries as well as five treatments for rabies. His most recent spider bite of note took place in Costa Rica, causing his right arm to swell up like an enormous kielbasa. BTG was awarded the Order of Australia in 2014 for his services to literature and wildlife conservation. He is happily married and currently divides his time between Australia and the United States in order to placate his parents and his American in-laws, though in truth he spends a great deal of time in a remote corner of Alaska avoiding them both.

Owl Fly (*Libelloides coccajus*)